BRITISH ARTISTS
Edited by John Rothenstein
Director and Keeper of the
Tate Gallery, London

WILSON STEER
by
Robin Ironside

WILSON STEER

BY
ROBIN IRONSIDE

LONDON: GEORGE ALLEN & UNWIN LTD
NEW YORK: THE OXFORD UNIVERSITY PRESS

PUBLISHED BY THE PHAIDON PRESS

ALL RIGHTS RESERVED · PUBLISHED BY THE PHAIDON PRESS
14 · ST GILES · OXFORD · AND 41 MUSEUM STREET · LONDON WC1

PRINTED IN 1943 BY
ROBERT MACLEHOSE AND COMPANY LIMITED, AT THE UNIVERSITY PRESS, GLASGOW

INTRODUCTION

THE ART OF STEER may be unhesitatingly placed in that category of English painting of which the frank vision of Constable has furnished the most conspicuous and lovely examples, a category to which Gainsborough, Crome, Bonington and David Cox also belong, one which can best be defined as displaying the fruits of an immediate unquestioning response to loved aspects of the visible world, furthermore a professional response, since it can be assumed that the sheer exercise of rendering it, whether rapidly or fluently, or with labour, is a preoccupation inseparable from the response itself, the impulse to paint, we may surmise being a component part of the delight experienced in the contemplation of nature; these artists are natural painters whose joy in appearances is unaffected. Such generalizations in the history and criticism of art are the more dangerous, being temptingly easy to make; for painting has flourished in 'schools' as music and literature have not. We must remember that the history of at least modern art is properly the history of artists; we may nevertheless speak of a category in this context, since it is possible to discover in the development of English painting two clear and divergent tendencies of which Constable naturally epitomizes the one and Blake as inevitably the other, the less pure and the more soulful. The poetry of Steer's vision is not only, however, simple to classify in this sense; it is perhaps the most complete instance in modern English painting of that coincidence of receptivity and skill which is the quality of the great natural, the great extravert painters. Among those of his own generation, we may include Sickert and Clausen, without unduly straining the classification, in the same pedigree together with many of the more modest lights of the New English Art Club, a movement of which Steer, however unconsciously, was the solar planet; among his successors any attempt to classify must be made warily, but at least we may divine something of that unhampered cultivation of a natural gift—unhampered, that is to say, by the compulsion of any pre-conceived images in the mind's eye—in the art

5

of Claude Rogers and Victor Pasmore. No contemporary English painter, however, has seemed to possess such a singleness of heart, such a freedom from the restraints of tendentiousness, almost, one might say, from the encroachments of the intellect, as are revealed in Steer's innocent and forthright art.

His powers were naturally, exclusively and serenely devoted to the development and expansion of his gift. Content with his vocation and intent upon its pursuit, there were consequently few external events in his life. He was born on December 28, 1860, at Birkenhead, the son of Philip Steer (1810-71), a portrait painter, and Emma Harrison. The family moved *c.* 1864 to Whitchurch in Herefordshire, where, as Frank Rutter has suggested, the neighbourhood of the Wye Valley, the rolling, fertile prospects of its scenery, may have first implanted in the painter—and at an age when impressions are gathered which become treasured recollections in later life —that love of the lucent expanses of pastoral and wooded country, that grasp of the pictorial possibilities of broad distant prospects of which the evidence in his mature work is so familiar. As a boy, Steer was sent to the Cathedral school at Hereford and later (at the age of sixteen) was placed with a private tutor, Dr. Purcell, at Whitchurch. He has said that he began to paint as early as he can remember; while still under Dr. Purcell, he was already versed in the practice of oil painting; his father's profession had accustomed him from an earlier age to the uses and materials of the craft; there seems indeed to have been no circumstance in his early life to impede the growth of a gift which was already his by nature and which, one must believe, so clearly are his pictures those of a born painter, an environment infinitely less auspicious would have failed to suppress. He was sent nevertheless to London to study for an Assistantship at the British Museum, though he never sat for the examination, choosing to return home where he became a student at the Gloucester Art School then under John Kemp. In the light of the opportunities it provided for absorbing the art of the past in so far as that was possible in the national collections—opportunities of which Steer took regular advantage—the time spent in London ought hardly to be considered as a pause in the development of his talent. In the autumn of 1882, having failed to enter the Royal Academy Schools, he went to Paris, where he worked at Julian's under Bouguereau and in 1883 at the Ecole des Beaux Arts under Cabanel in whose teaching he had some confidence. He returned to London in 1884 as a result of the imposition of a rule, with which he felt unable to comply, that all foreigners at the Ecole des Beaux Arts should be required to pass an examination in French, a reaction illustrating the pronounced strain of English conservatism in his personality and his aversion from other studies than that of painting.

The instinctive nationalism of his character may have contributed to the lack of fervour with which he responded to acquaintance with the French Impressionist School of which he was first made aware at an exhibition in London, in the early 80's, at Messrs. Dowdeswells, a school of which his own pictures were to present the most truly English counterpart. His youthful enthusiasms were for Burne-Jones (particularly the *Pygmalion* series), and for Watts and Millais; he felt the quality of Whistler, but considered his paintings too misty. It is consequently less surprising that he received somewhat mildly the Memorial Exhibition of Manet's works held in Paris in 1883, though it was in his own rising talent that George Moore was later to find consolation for Manet's death. Mr. Collins Baker has recorded that the exhibition impressed him but not greatly; that he felt that Manet, of whom he had never heard before, was 'something entirely different . . . but did not like the pictures: he thought they looked curiously swollen—pneumatic so to speak'. 'The Nudes', he told Mr. John Rothenstein, 'looked blown out.' His paintings alone, however, would show that, whatever his first feelings, his sensibilities absorbed and profited by the lessons, both in vision and technique which French Impressionism dictated. The growth of their influence was doubtless hastened by an Impressionist Exhibition at the Goupil Gallery in 1889. Steer was profoundly effected by these lessons without being in the least intellectually converted to a system. While in Paris, his ignorance of French hindered or preserved him from floating among the lively cross-currents of thought which were then agitating artistic circles. His companions were Edward Stott, T. B. Kennington, one of the Dalziels and James Christie. Even had he been able to mix freely and strike friendships among French painters and art students, it is difficult to imagine that he would have given real attention to the banners under which they grouped themselves; slumber was often his response to the conversation of George Moore, Tonks and D. S. MacColl. He never had any inclination towards abstract thinking. A critic writing in *The Times* has justly remarked that he responded to the influence of French Impressionism 'as a matter of course and without a trace of theoretical acquiescence'. His gift appears to have opened almost heedlessly under that light, like a plant under the sun's rays.

He began exhibiting at the Academy (1883) while he was still a student in Paris. His second exhibit was sold before the date of opening; he was subsequently skied and rejected in succession, after which he refrained from submitting further works.* In 1886, the new English Art Club was founded, a body which united those tendencies in British painting which conflicted both with the traditions encouraged at the Academy (unavailingly among most of its exhibitors), and the mystic aestheticism of Watts, Rossetti and Burne-Jones. Steer was one of the original members and without any doubt among the finest of its regular exhibitors. Notwithstanding the influence and support of Whistler, the character of the Club was above all else naturalist; it represented a movement which sought to give pictorial expression to work-a-day subject matter, to present landscape as it is ordinarily perceived out of doors; it was aesthetic only in so far as it valued qualities of rendering and handling and the sensory acuteness of the artists' vision, qualities for which, too often, we may seek in vain among the work of the run of its adherents. Flights of poetic imagination were beyond the range of its general outlook; pictures of fancy, however, were painted by members of the Club and so far as there was any sentimental bias, this tended to express, without idealization, a social realist compassion and esteem for the life of the peasant and worker, a touched interest in the ups and downs of ordinary existence. A similar attitude has been given noble expression by Millet; the inspiration reflected in the subject pictures of those painters properly within the orbit of the new English Art Club was, however, more nearly akin to that of the mediocre, less grave and more forced interpretations of Bastien Lepage; the prevailing tone of their landscape was pleinairist rather than in direct relation to the great impressionists. By 1886, in Paris, the symbolists were already succeeding the impressionists as a novel focus of interest. But it was not till

* Until 1940 when he was persuaded to send a water-colour to the annual exhibition.

1889 that an exhibition of London Impressionists was held; it might have been less remarkable had it been held in 1839. The history of art is anything but a history of progress: that English painting, however, which, by the example of Constable and Turner, had delighted and inspired Monet and Pissarro, should dissipate part of its energy upon putting forth a homely but faint reflection of a landscape school which, to a measurable extent, was its debtor, disposes of any claim that is advanced on behalf of the principle proclivities of the new English Art Club that they gave coherence to the forward tendencies in English Painting or rescued our art from stagnation in other directions.* But it can be said that, because, as a liberally managed institution, the Club accepted much that the Academy would not, an important proportion of the vigorous and independent talent in which the live current of English art was henceforward to be born, was made public at its exhibitions.

Critical remarks upon the historical implications of the New English Art Club may be supposed out of place in discussing the art of a painter so remote from theoretical pre-occupations. But it is necessary to make them if only because Steer's close association with the Club must give it, as representing a movement, a lustre which it would not otherwise deserve. His landscape does not deliberately aspire to a condition beyond that which most of his fellow exhibitors trusted to reach. Nature and the tradition of Constable and Turner are the supports upon which it knowingly leans, impressionism, it may be said, having re-emphasized their claims to study by an Englishman; Steer rose at once far above the average level of the exhibitors at the New English, not because his motives were remarkable, but because his impressions were intense while theirs were flat, and because his manner flowed out his impressions, however steeped in tradition these may have been. He was represented at the first exhibition of the Club and it was through its agency that his reputation grew; it became, in a sense, the platform of his art and his loyalty to it was consistent. From the time of its foundation onwards, there are few biographical facts concerning him to record. Nature and tra-

*The work of Conder, Beardsley, Rothenstein, and John, all of whom exhibited at the N.E.A.C., cannot be associated with the pervading impressionistic tendencies of the Club; the same may be said of the early work of McEvoy. Sickert was an exhibitor but subsequently seceded.

dition took their course, unobstructed, with his talent, which flowered without interruption and with a fine evenness until the tragedy of failing sight obliged him to relinquish the practice of the art to which he had consecrated himself entirely. In spite of the early misunderstanding of critics, his reputation grew almost as smoothly as his gift, D. S. MacColl and George Moore being eloquent, early and victorious in the defence and appreciation of his work. The veneration in which it has since long been publicly held was not born of any limelight; while inevitably aloof from academic circles, while remaining fundamentally an independent, and in some ways a recluse, official recognition came to him, unsolicited but welcome, through the medium of his painting alone and of the simplicity of its message. It is the more difficult to conceive how a critic of the 80's, confronted for the first time by Steer's pictures, the value of which however original they may be, has never resided in their novelty, could complain that 'life and thought have gone away, side by side.'

The influence of the French is most conspicuous in his work of the late 80's and early 90's; a suggestion of Monet is charmingly present in the exquisite series of seaside views executed during this period; the *Pierhead at Walberswick* (1888), *The Ermine Sea* (1890), *Boulogne Sands* (1892), *Yachts* (1893, Tate Gallery), and *Children Paddling* (1894), have something both of the sparkle and the limpidity of Monet's vision. In the portraits of this time, we may discern the effect of Degas' and of Manet's example, of the former in *Mrs. Cyprian Williams* (1890-91) and *Self-Portrait with a Model*, and of the latter in *Jennie Lee* (1889). At the same time, such portraits as *Head of Girl* (1893) reveal a reliance on the elegance of Whistler which, indeed, is also noticeable in the svelte, adolescent forms of the girls in the *Pierhead at Walberswick* and *Children Running on a Pier* (1894). Steer seems to have responded to the achievements of other masters in much the same manner as he responded to nature; there is no trace either of affectation or base imitation in his adoption of the modes of the modern masters or in the support which he has justly and unashamedly accepted from the old; a clear grasp and sympathetic use of the achievements of those painters whom he naturally admired is in regular evidence throughout his work.

Towards the close of the eighteen-nineties, the direct influence upon his vision of Whistler and the impressionists waned; the tenuous grace of his early figure painting, the evanescent quality, the comparatively transparent surfaces of the landscapes of the same period are encountered less frequently. From approximately 1900, the forms swell, become encrusted and substantial; the area of vision opens out, the motifs, whether persons or landscapes, have a more majestic aspect. The finest pictures of this mature phase are heavy with colour; their impasto, applied often with a knife, is rich and prominent. There is no renunciation of impressionism, but an endeavour to graft its discoveries upon the landscape manner sanctified by European, particularly English, tradition, not by introducing a monumental, impassive formality beneath the surface glitter, but by balancing this within the ample rhythms of traditional composition. The gain in strength and nobility was counterbalanced by the loss—never afterwards fully compensated—of a very personal element of poetic capriciousness in colour and conception which is peculiarly delightful in the early seaside pictures. The masters who now chiefly inspired his landscape were Constable, Gainsborough and Rubens; *Richmond Castle* (1903), the paintings of Chepstow Castle (1905-6) and Poole Harbour (1908), can fittingly be compared with Constable's full-size sketches; the park-like atmosphere of Gainsborough's later landscapes pervades his vision of the groves of Bridgnorth and Knaresborough, while *The Rainbow* (1901) is an unmistakable echo of Rubens.

It has been suggested that the conversation pieces of Tonks had some influence upon Steer's portraits and genre subjects of this period and a relationship, if not an influence, is evident in such works as Steer's *Music Room* (1905-6) or *the Balcony* (1909, Johannesburg). Whatever the effect of Tonks' paintings, his personality and views certainly affected Steer's practice; the Pre-Raphaelite finish, however, which he admired, but misapprehended, was out of tune with the grace and breadth of Steer's natural manner; *the Muslin Dress* (1910) and *the End of the Chapter* (1911), both reflecting the teaching of Tonks, are incongruously over-realized and are touched with that hesitant sentimentality which mars much, if not all, of Tonks' work. It is interesting to note that these pictures, and also *Hydrangeas* (1901) which may be grouped with them are reminiscent of the semi-Pre-Raphaelite, Albert Moore, admired by Whistler from whom Steer had already gleaned so much. Under other inspiration, Steer's figure painting has prospered more happily; the full length of Mrs. Hammersley (1907) has the largeness of conception and the poise of a Gainsborough; and there is a genuine, picturesque feeling in such pictures as *Sleep* and the earlier *Toilet of Venus* (1898) in which Steer gives way to that nostalgia for the piquant gallantries of the eighteenth century which affected the arts at the very end of the nineteenth, largely propagated by the Goncourts and appearing in England in the art of Conder and Beardsley. Steer's portraits and subject pictures are, however, normally inferior to his landscape; his draughtsmanship has a looseness and his perception of character an unpenetrating simplicity which inevitably hinder him as a portraitist, his most beautiful achievement in this field being the portrait of his old housekeeper, Mrs. Raynes, painted as late as 1922; here, his intimate knowledge of the sitter, his affection, even reverence, for her character, gave the work the character of a tribute; the picture radiates sympathy and understanding as no other portrait from his hand.

The progress of Steer's painting cannot be divided into distinct phases; but it may be said that towards 1913, the effects of the example of Turner upon his work are more marked than before. The Harwich views (1913), and those of Chelsea Embankment (c. 1913-18) are thinly painted, liquid visions, recalling Turner's latest unexhibited work, (also Monet's Thames subjects), and contrast with the mottled, weighty surfaces of *Richmond Castle* or *The Rainbow*. This Turnerian manner can be studied at its finest in the lovely group of Shoreham subjects painted in the nineteen-twenties. They have the vagueness, the swimming quality of water-colour and are closely related in treatment to similar subjects by the painter in this medium. Steer's water-colour art, which failing eyesight impelled him to cultivate increasingly in recent years, is essentially traditionalist like his work in oil, but it presents a combination of the elements of tradition which is more rarely found in his oil paintings.

Tonks saw in it a faint touch of the oriental, added to a pure English tradition. Echoes—often somewhat muffled—of the Japanese, hints of Turner and of the 'blots' of Alexander Cozens, mingle in the same drawing. Certain recurrent effects of *tachisme*, however, also suggest the inspiration of Claude. Steer was painting in water-colour at least as early as 1900, but it was not until 1918, when his proficiency in this medium made a marked forward stride, that he devoted to it that almost dogged attention which has since been so richly justified. But it must be said that the quality of his water-colour style, intermittently a beautiful one, fails when compared with the more laborious structure of the oils. Steer worked rapidly in water-colour and only a small proportion of the results of a summer painting tour were preserved and mounted by him. Not all of these possess that felicity of utterance without which a spontaneity is of no avail. The shapes of which they are composed are sometimes both uninformative and limp in themselves; the extreme generalization of the subject matter, at times full of what seems an instinctive subtlety, at other less illuminated moments might have been the outcome as much of the waywardness of the medium as the handling of the painter. It would, on the other hand, be superfluous to point out that they are evidence of a singleness of purpose enabling him to overcome, in later life, the obstacle of a weakening sight by the cultivation to a remarkable pitch of skill of a summary method of expression—though it is indeed a tribute to the man that this obstacle was thus defeated. At their best they are limpid examples of a branch of art for which English painting has proved itself peculiarly gifted, and more than uphold the standards of the native tradition. To name particular drawings such as *Alum Bay* (Whitworth Art Gallery, Manchester) for its seemingly fugitive grace, or *Misty Morning on the Severn* (1925) for its transparent depths would be an arbitrary proceeding. Water-colours floated off his brush in a swift stream; many of them are very slight and they are most beautiful when seen in conjunction with one another. In various company, the particular charm of the shorthand employed tends to be less easily discernible, the drenched, often subdued quality of the colour to evaporate. Assembled with care, they can be seen to be the fruits of a subtle and consistent vision, one which can bathe a room in a liquid reflection of the moods of nature.

Though Steer was no novel experimenter, though his work displays undisguisedly the pleased surrender of his sensibilities to whatever qualities were admirable in those masters whom he most revered, we can yet point to the singularity of his landscape art, to that loving handling of the great commonplaces of an Englishman's delight in nature, a branch of the national sentiment of which, in the recent history of painting, Steer's has been the only sonorous voice. In the foam-flecked pools bathing the feet of his paddling children, shallows of an 'opium blue, the blue of an oblivion', George Moore has written, '. . . which fades and deepens imperceptibly, like a flower from the intense heart to the delicate edge of the petals,' in the gentle inrush of the waves of his Ermine Sea, or the airy languours that seem to flutter off the waters at evening beyond the pierhead at Walberswick, the painter has gathered up all the entranced sensations of youthful visits to the seaside. Of the vast country prospects which he has unrolled, though they are without the sweetness and the sharpness of the earlier paintings, we can say that they break upon our view in a kind of naked beauty as when a bend in the road or a lifting of the mist suddenly reveals a wonderful and unsuspected vista; they are glimpses, though majestic and essential, of the poetry of our most spacious scenery. At their most serene, as especially in the two *Golden Valleys*, there hovers over them the faint aura of an earthly paradise; one would not say, however, that the quality of Steer's landscape vision is primarily elysian. It does not normally do more than perceive the unalloyed beauties of nature, but these are translated for us so wholeheartedly, at the beginning with an affectionate solicitude and later with such a simple and grandiloquent verve, that our pulses are quickened by the painter's response, to all appearances swift and instinctive, to the changeful aspects of this island in which the sea, whose neighbourhood is pervasive, strikes everywhere a chime, adding a marine freshness to the most inland regions. Steer's landscape art at its best is always the flattering mirror of our least complex pleasures in the presence of nature. Great groves of trees at Bridgnorth are presented without comment, but with a superior understanding of their inherent strength and exuberance; dramatic effects of the sun upon Richmond or Chepstow Castle are rendered without self-conscious dramatization by the artist, but with the most vivid apprehension of the unexpected hues created by the shifting light and weather. Light and weather are indeed the constant muses of his work as they are the chief architects of those natural splendours which are most generally loved; the familiar majesty of cumulus has rarely been more completely expressed than in *Poole Harbour* or the subtleties of colour, which we detect in the blond morning haze which seeps over the shore from the Channel, been deciphered with such a penetrating glance as in the diaphanous series of sea and shore-scapes painted by Steer at Shoreham.

That we are recurringly reminded as we survey his achievement, though with rarely a hint of pastiche, of the peculiar vision of Turner, Constable or Gainsborough serves merely to unite him openly and unaffectedly with our established heritage of landscape painting. There is a progressive Toryism about his art which effectively shielded him from the dangers, noble though these are, of experimentalism and prevented, with the aid of Manet and Monet, the attractive sanctuary of Constable and Turner from obscuring the evidence of his eyes or captivating him in stylistic formulae. His art subsists evergreen in our midst, at a time when painting is seeking increasingly a new romance in the regions of personality, because it is a powerful, unobjectionable expression, without complexity, safe in the lack of any personal philosophic or literary motives, motives which may lift an artist to greatness, but which may also, where his gifts in this sphere are unequal, sow pitfalls for a talent which might otherwise flourish within less ambitious limits. No landscape of Steer's displays the pantomime atmosphere of some of Turner's exhibited pictures; equally, none competes with the transcendent quality of, among many wonderful examples, *The Evening Star* on the late *Norham Castle*. Steer was mostly content, without enquiring into Nature's deeper influences on the human spirit, with a frank and pure pursuit of her loveliness.

SEASCAPE. Oil. Fitzwilliam Museum, Cambridge

15

ACKNOWLEDGMENTS

THE EDITOR wishes to record his thanks to all those owners of pictures by Steer who have facilitated the reproduction of works in their collections and particularly to Sir Augustus Daniel and the late Geoffrey Blackwell, O.B.E. ; the author is indebted to Mr. Ronald Gray and Mr. Lockett Thomson for valuable help in tracing and dating pictures and to Mr. A. M. Hind for placing at his disposal the catalogues and biographical material compiled by Mr. C. H. Collins Baker and the late Isherwood Kay and now preserved in the Department of Prints and Drawings at the British Museum.

PORTRAIT OF ELEANOR LARKIN
Miniature. 1897.
Collection of Lady Kendall Butler

LIST OF THE PLATES

I. OIL PAINTINGS

1. A DEAD BULLFINCH. $6'' \times 9\frac{3}{4}''$. Painted when the artist was fifteen. Collection of Major W. R. Hornby Steer

2. THE ALPS AT EARL'S COURT. $30'' \times 25''$. The Tate Gallery.

3. COWES REGATTA. 1892. $20'' \times 24''$. Collection of John Scaramanga, Esq.

4. BEACH SCENE WITH CHILDREN PADDLING. $18\frac{3}{4}'' \times 22\frac{1}{2}''$. Collection of Sir A. M. Daniel, K.B.E.

5. KNUCKLEBONES, WALBERSWICK. 1888. $24\frac{1}{2}'' \times 30\frac{1}{4}''$. Collection of Herbert West, Esq.

6. DOLLY BROWN, WALBERSWICK. In the artist's possession in 1941.

7. MADAME ZOZO IN 'DRESDINA'. 1889. $23\frac{1}{2}'' \times 30''$. Collection of Sir A. M. Daniel, K.B.E.

8. THE PIER HEAD, WALBERSWICK. 1888. $36'' \times 36''$. Collection of Hugo Pitman, Esq.

9. THE BRIDGE AT ETAPLES. 1887. $18\frac{3}{4}'' \times 25\frac{1}{4}''$. The Tate Gallery.

10. PORTRAIT OF JENNIE LEE. 1889. $36'' \times 28''$. Collection of Mrs. Clifton.

11. JONQUILS. $36'' \times 36''$. Collection of Mr. Pilling.

12. POOLE HARBOUR. 1890. $24\frac{1}{2}'' \times 18\frac{5}{8}''$. Collection of Sir Edward Marsh, K.C.V.O., C.B., C.M.G.

13. CHILDREN PADDLING. 1894. $25'' \times 36''$. Collection of Sir A. M. Daniel, K.B.E.

14. A SUNLIT SEA. $23\frac{1}{4}'' \times 29\frac{1}{2}''$. Collection of Hugo Pitman, Esq.

15. BOULOGNE SANDS. 1892. $24'' \times 30''$. Collection of Miss Ellen Brown.

16. HEAD OF A GIRL. 1893. $10\frac{1}{4}'' \times 8''$. Present owner unknown.

17. THE MIRROR, 1894. $37'' \times 20''$. Adams Gallery, London.

18. MRS. CYPRIAN WILLIAMS AND CHILDREN. 1890-91. $30'' \times 40''$. The Tate Gallery.

19. SELF-PORTRAIT WITH MODEL. 24" × 12". Collection of Dermod O'Brien, Esq.

20. THE MAUVE DRESS. 20½" × 16½". The City Art Gallery, Manchester.

21. BUST PORTRAIT OF A YOUNG WOMAN. 25" × 23½". Collection of Sir A. M. Daniel, K.B.E.

22. THE BEACH AT WALBERSWICK. 1890. 23¼" × 29⅝". The Tate Gallery.

23. THE ERMINE SEA. 1890. 24" × 30". Collection of Sir A. M. Daniel, K.B.E.

24. CHILDREN RUNNING ON A PIER. 1894. 23¾" × 35½". Collection of Sir A. M. Daniel, K.B.E.

25. PORTRAIT OF MISS ETHEL DIXON BEFORE A MIRROR. 20½" × 16½". No. 172 in the Steer Sale, Christie's, London, July 1942.

26. CHINCHILLA. 24" × 20". In the artist's possession in 1941.

27. LUDLOW CASTLE WITH STORMY SKY. 1896. 19" × 25". Collection of Sir A. M. Daniel, K.B.E.

28. A VIEW OF EASEBY ABBEY. 1895. 23½" × 35". Collection of Major W. R. Hornby Steer.

29. STUDY FOR 'THE TOILET OF VENUS'. 30" × 25". Collection of the Duchess of Roxburghe.

30. THE TOILET OF VENUS. 1898. 100" × 72". The Tate Gallery.

31. A GIRL SEATED AT NEEDLEWORK. Pastel. 1889. 24½" × 18½". Collection of the Viscount Bearsted, M.C.

32. WOMAN IN A WHITE BLOUSE SEATED ON A SOFA. 1899. 29" × 24". Collection of Sir A. M. Daniel, K.B.E.

33. SLEEP. 35" × 52". The Tate Gallery.

34. TWO NUDE WOMEN WITH A MIRROR. 1901. 15" × 21". Collection of Sir A. M. Daniel, K.B.E.

35. HYDRANGEAS. 1901. 34" × 44". Collection of John Scaramanga, Esq.

36. THE SEVERN ('GOLDEN') VALLEY. 1902. 25¾" × 30¾". Collection of the Rt. Hon. Vincent Massey, P.C.

37. THE GOLDEN VALLEY. 26" × 31". 1902. Collection of Sir A. M. Daniel, K.B.E.

38. THE HOME FARM. 1901. 22" × 27". Collection of the late Geoffrey Blackwell, O.B.E.

39. THE RAINBOW. 1901. 20" × 33". Collection of the late Geoffrey Blackwell, O.B.E.

II. WATERCOLOURS

CHRONOLOGICAL LIST

OF PLACES AT WHICH THE ARTIST WORKED

1884 WALBERSWICK
1885 WALBERSWICK?
1886 WALBERSWICK?
1887 DANNES, NEAR ÉTAPLES
1888 BOULOGNE (?)
1889 MONTREUIL-SUR-MER, ALSO
WALBERSWICK
1890 SWANAGE
1891 BOULOGNE—SHORT VISITS TO DIFFERENT PLACES
INCLUDING HAYLING ISLAND
1892 COWES
1893 RICHMOND, SURREY
1894 BOULOGNE AND RYE?
1895 RICHMOND, YORKSHIRE
1896 BARNARD CASTLE
1897 KNARESBOROUGH
1898 LUDLOW
1899 LUDLOW
1900 KNARESBOROUGH
1901 BRIDGNORTH
1902 STROUD
1903 RICHMOND, YORKSHIRE
1904 HAWES, YORKSHIRE
1905 CHEPSTOW
1906 LUDLOW
1907 MONTREUIL-SUR-MER
1908 CORFE
1909 NEWNHAM AND LITTLEDEAN
1910 IRONBRIDGE
1911 BRIDGNORTH
1912 PORCHESTER
1913 HARWICH
1914 BOSHAM
1915 PAINSWICK
1916 CHIRK
1917 CHIRK
1918 DOVER
1919 ALUM BAY, ISLE OF WIGHT
1920 MALDON
1921 HYTHE, SOUTHAMPTON WATER
1922 SHIREHAMPTON, NEAR BRISTOL
1923 BRILL
1924 LONG CRENDON
1925 BRIDGNORTH
1926 SHOREHAM, SUSSEX
1928 FRAMLINGHAM
1929 HARWICH
1930 DOVER
1931 WHITSTABLE AND SANDWICH
1932 GREENHITHE
1933 MALDON
1934 WALMER

21

THE PLATES

1. A DEAD BULLFINCH. Painted when the artist was fifteen. Collection of Major W. R. Hornby Steer

2. THE ALPS AT EARL'S COURT. The Tate Gallery

3. COWES REGATTA. 1892. Collection of John Scaramanga, Esq.

4. BEACH SCENE WITH CHILDREN PADDLING. Collection of Sir A. M. Daniel, K.B.E.

5. KNUCKLEBONES, WALBERSWICK. 1888. Collection of Herbert West, Esq.

6. DOLLY BROWN, WALBERSWICK. In the artist's possession in 1941

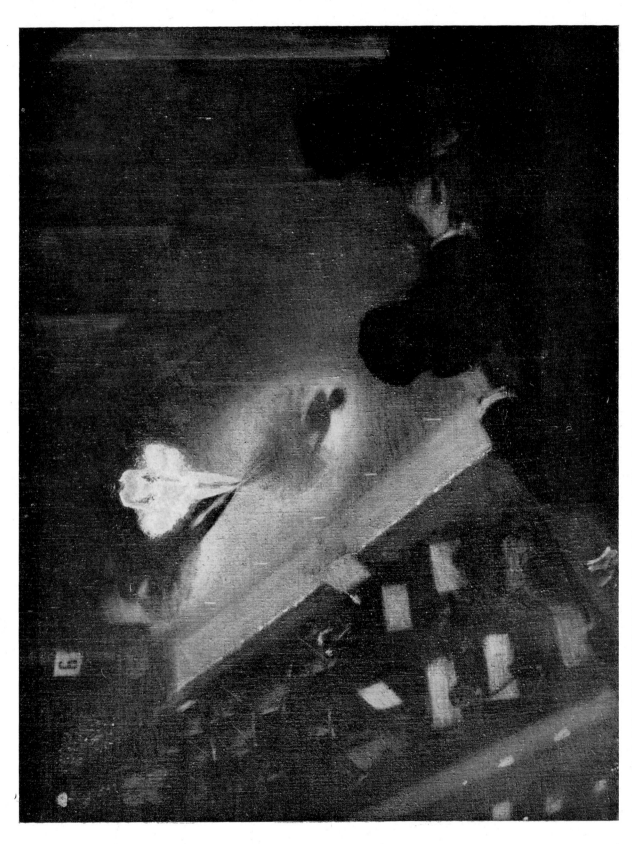

7. MADAME ZOZO IN 'DRESDINA'. 1889. Collection of Sir A. M. Daniel, K.B.E.

8. THE PIER HEAD, WALBERSWICK. 1888. Collection of Hugo Pitman, Esq.

9. THE BRIDGE AT ETAPLES. 1887. The Tate Gallery

10. PORTRAIT OF JENNIE LEE. 1889. Collection of Mrs. Clifton

11. JONQUILS. Collection of Mr. Pilling

12. POOLE HARBOUR. 1890. Collection of Sir Edward Marsh, K.C.V.O., C.B., C.M.G.

13. CHILDREN PADDLING. 1894. Collection of Sir A. M. Daniel, K.B.E.

14. A SUNLIT SEA. Collection of Hugo Pitman, Esq.

15. BOULOGNE SANDS. 1892. Collection of Miss Ellen Brown

16. HEAD OF A GIRL. 1893. Present owner unknown   17. THE MIRROR, 1894. Adams Gallery, London
18. MRS. CYPRIAN WILLIAMS AND CHILDREN. 1890-91. The Tate Gallery

19. SELF-PORTRAIT WITH MODEL. Collection of Dermod O'Brien, Esq.

20. THE MAUVE DRESS. The City Art Gallery, Manchester

21. BUST PORTRAIT OF A YOUNG WOMAN. Collection of Sir A. M. Daniel, K.B.E.

22. THE BEACH AT WALBERSWICK. 1890. The Tate Gallery

23. THE ERMINE SEA. 1890. Collection of Sir A. M. Daniel, K.B.E.

24. CHILDREN RUNNING ON A PIER. 1894. Collection of Sir A. M. Daniel, K.B.E.

25. PORTRAIT OF MISS ETHEL DIXON BEFORE A MIRROR. No. 172 in the Steer Sale, Christie's,
London, July 1942

26. CHINCHILLA. In the artist's possession in 1941

27. LUDLOW CASTLE WITH STORMY SKY. 1896. Collection of Sir A. M. Daniel, K.B.E.

28. A VIEW OF EASEBY ABBEY. 1895. Collection of Major W. R. Hornby Steer

G

29. STUDY FOR 'THE TOILET OF VENUS'. Collection of the Duchess of Roxburghe

30. THE TOILET OF VENUS. 1898. The Tate Gallery

31. A GIRL SEATED AT NEEDLEWORK. Pastel. 1889. Collection of the Viscount Bearsted, M.C.

32. WOMAN IN A WHITE BLOUSE SEATED ON A SOFA. 1899. Collection of Sir A. M. Daniel, K.B.E.

33. SLEEP. The Tate Gallery

34. TWO NUDE WOMEN WITH A MIRROR. 1901. Collection of Sir A. M. Daniel, K.B.E.

35. HYDRANGEAS. 1901. Collection of John Scaramanga, Esq.

36. THE SEVERN ('GOLDEN') VALLEY. 1902. Collection of the Rt. Hon. Vincent Massey, P.C.

37. THE GOLDEN VALLEY. 1902. Collection of Sir A. M. Daniel, K.B.E.

38. THE HOME FARM. 1901. Collection of the late Geoffrey Blackwell, O.B.E.

H

39. THE RAINBOW. 1901. Collection of the late Geoffrey Blackwell, O.B.E.

40. RICHMOND CASTLE. 1903. The Tate Gallery

41. WATERFALL AT RICHMOND, YORKSHIRE: AN AUTUMNAL EVENING. The Beaux Arts Gallery, London

42. RICHMOND: THE SHOWER. 1903. Collection of the late Geoffrey Blackwell, O.B.E.

43. THE WYE AT CHEPSTOW. 1905. The Walker Art Gallery, Liverpool

44. EVENING, LUDLOW. The Ashmolean Museum, Oxford

45. CHEPSTOW CASTLE. 1906. *Reproduced by gracious permission of H.M. The Queen*

46. CHEPSTOW CASTLE. 1905. The Tate Gallery

47. THE MUSIC ROOM. 1905-6. The Tate Gallery

48. MRS. HAMMERSLEY. 1907. Collection of Mrs. Hammersley

49. THE ISLE OF PURBECK. Collection of the late Geoffrey Blackwell, O.B.E.

50. OUTSKIRTS OF A TOWN. 1907. Collection of George Healing, Esq.

51. THE HORSESHOE BEND OF THE SEVERN. 1909. The City Art Gallery, Manchester

52. LUDLOW: SCENE IN A PARK. 1909. Collection of the late Geoffrey Blackwell, O.B.E.

53. THE HORSESHOE BEND OF THE SEVERN. 1909. The Art Gallery, Aberdeen

54. BRIDGNORTH. August 17, 1917. Collection of Sir A. M. Daniel, K.B.E.

K

55. POOLE HARBOUR. 1908. Collection of Captain Jeremy Pemberton

56. BRIDGNORTH. 1911. Collection of John Scaramanga, Esq.

57. OUTSKIRTS OF A TOWN. The Ashmolean Museum, Oxford

58. THE MUSLIN DRESS. 1910. Collection of the Viscount Leverhulme

59. THE END OF THE CHAPTER. 1911. The Art Gallery, Bradford

60. GOLDEN EVENING. 1914. The City Art Gallery, Leeds

61. THE TOY BOAT. 1899. Collection of Colonel and Mrs. Tetley

62. GATHERING SEAWEED. Begun in 1913; finished in 1934. Collection of the Rt. Hon. Vincent Massey, P.C.

L

63. AMONG THE TREES, BRIDGNORTH. Collection of the late Geoffrey Blackwell, O.B.E.

64. SELF-PORTRAIT. Collection of Sir A. M. Daniel, K.B.E.

65. MRS. RAYNES. 1922. The Tate Gallery

66. DOVER HARBOUR. 1918. The Imperial War Museum

67. A SHIPYARD, SHOREHAM. 1926. Messrs. Ernest Brown and Phillips Ltd. London

68. DIGGING FOR BAIT; SHOREHAM. 1926. The Art Gallery, the Civic Centre, Southampton

69. THE CREEK: KINGSTON. 1926. Collection of Sir A. M. Daniel, K.B.E.

70. CASTLE AND LAKE. Watercolour. 1903. The Fitzwilliam Museum, Cambridge

71. STORMY SKY, NEAR STROUD. Watercolour. 1902. Collection of H. C. Laurence, Esq.

72. NEAR RICHMOND, YORKSHIRE. Watercolour. 1903. Collection of H. C. Laurence, Esq.

73. BRIDGNORTH, WATERCOLOUR. 1925. Collection of the late Geoffrey Blackwell, O.B.E.

74. MISTY MORNING ON THE SEVERN. Watercolour. 1925. Collection of H. C. Laurence, Esq.

75. HOUSES AMONG TREES. Watercolour. In the artist's possession in 1941

76. THE SEA AT WALMER. Watercolour. 1934. In the artist's possession in 1941

77. MALDON QUAY. Watercolour. 1920. Collection of Herbert West, Esq.

78. MALDON, LOW TIDE. Watercolour. 1933. Collection of H. C. Laurence, Esq.

INDEX OF COLLECTIONS

PORTRAIT SKETCH OF WILSON STEER. 1915
Pencil drawing by Ina Sheldon-Williams
British Museum